JOHN BUTLER-HOPKINS

FOR THE LOVE OF POETRY

With best wishes

John Butler Hopkins

AUSTIN MACAULEY PUBLISHERS™
LONDON • CAMBRIDGE • NEW YORK • SHARJAH

Copyright © John Butler-Hopkins 2022

The right of John Butler-Hopkins to be identified as author of this work has been asserted in accordance with sections 77 and 78 of the Copyright, Designs and Patents Act 1988.

All rights reserved. No part of this publication may be reproduced, stored in a retrieval system, or transmitted in any form or by any means, electronic, mechanical, photocopying, recording, or otherwise, without the prior permission of the publishers.

Any person who commits any unauthorised act in relation to this publication may be liable to criminal prosecution and civil claims for damages.

A CIP catalogue record for this title is available from the British Library.

ISBN 9781398476295 (Paperback)
ISBN 9781398476301 (Hardback)
ISBN 9781398476318 (ePub e-book)

www.austinmacauley.com

First Published 2022
Austin Macauley Publishers Ltd
1 Canada Square
Canary Wharf
London
E14 5AA

To my partner Glenda for her constant encouragement.

Poems

Destiny	7
My England	8
Powers of Nature/Glory of Creation	9
Rhapsody of Love	10
Bridge of Love's Desire	11
Masquerade of Love	12
Heart of Stone	13
Red Roses	14
Under a Cloud to Hide the Moon	15
Writing's on the Wall	16
Forgive Me	17
One Day at a Time	18
Words of a Down and Out	19
Walking the Pavement	20
Someone Like You	21
Fascination	22
Long Before I Saw You	23
My Heart Didn't Need to Tell Me	24
Come with Me, My Love	25
Miss Tinkle Toes	26
The Dread of Cancer	27
Living with Cancer	28
White Feathers	29
Why Does It Have to Be?	30
If Only	31
Every Now and Then	32
You Were Love	33
In the Ashes of Our Love	34
Images of Love	35
Reminiscence	36
Painted Pictures on the Mind	37
Tragedy of War: WWI	38
The Conscript	39
We Were the Young Lads	40

One in Khaki, One in Grey	42
Pawns of Grief	43
Red Runs the Sky	44
Rain Marks Time	45
Demons in Grey	46
Ceasefire	47
Unknown Perils	48
Silent Harp	49
Prince of Youth	50
Virgin Snowdrop	51
Son of Love	52
Forever Young	53
Love Instead of Hate	54
Path of Eagles	55
Where No Birds Sing	56
Fields of Sorrow/Fields of Glory	57
Requiem	58
Village Memorial	59
The Barley Field	60
Remembrance Day	61
THE LOST LETTERS (SET TO POETRY)	**63**
When First We Met	64
When the Days Were Ours	65
Whisperings	66
Together We Will Be	67
Yesterdays	68
Buttercup Meadow	69
Winter Lace	70
Sweet Marjorie	71
Until We Meet Again	72
Killed in Action	73
Will You Remember Me	74
In Remembrance	75
Skeleton of Despair	76
Primrose Wood	77

Destiny

Another war to end all wars,
Another Pontius Pilate
To be waiting in the wings:
Just in case Christ
Should come back again.

With the seed of life
A new generation born
To follow its fate:
Richman, poor man,
Beggar man, thief:
Preordained destiny
To proclaim.

My England

I've travelled far and wide,
Seen places I could only image
In books and magazines,
When growing up from a child.

For every journey I take
Return to my birth place,
To breathe in the sea air
Standing on the cliff tops.

In a moment of nostalgia,
Hear the whistle blow
Of an old steam train,
Wearily plodding along its track
In a welcoming, back home.

To look above, at the skies around,
Where the 'Battle of Britain'
Was fought and won.
Say a prayer beneath my breath,
In memory of those gallant few
That gave their all.

For when the war was over
Being an evacuee, like in the song,
To sleep in my own little room again:
Where the white cliffs of Dover
Look out to sea.

Upon a hill side the castle stands,
Guarding the gateway to England
Ever steadfast,
Defiant to its enemy
Loyal unto the Crown.

Powers of Nature/Glory of Creation

Transformation in perfection
In unsurpassed beauty
Blooms the petals of a rose:
To fill the air
On its fragrance divine,
Beyond compare.

In unrivalled precision
Finely spun
A flimsy spider's web:
Defies the elements
In the outrage of storm,
To gently flow a summer breeze.

Transformation in perfection
On rain's aftermath:
For the colours of the rainbow,
Set into a perfect arch,
Taunt an envious sky.

For the will-o'-the-wisp
With its fluorescent glow
To dance the evening marshes:
On the silence of a prayer,
Skip the gravestones alongside
A forsaken church, of time left behind.

Powers of Nature, Glory of Creation.

Rhapsody of Love

On a moon-drenched shore
In grasped hands, to run naked,
Into the open arms
Of the calm upon the sea,
Where to wrap you in
'The Rhapsody of Love'.

Where after, to lay on a deserted beach,
Make love beneath the gathering twilight:
For two hearts entwined, beat in time
With the murmuring of the waves,
To look into each other's eyes upon
'The Rhapsody of Love'.

While on a dawn chorus of the birds
Welcoming in the day,
In bare feet to shouts of joy
Run a meadow wet with dew
Amongst the buttercups and daisies,
To enfold you in
'The Rhapsody of Love'.

For in the pouring rain
Dance beneath a rainbow,
Do all the wondrous things
That enchant the mind:
For two hearts in love
To pluck the chords
Upon a harp to play
'The Rhapsody of Love'.

Bridge of Love's Desire

On Bridge of Love's Desire
For the moon on high
To reflect its romantic glow,
Into the calm, clear waters
That flow beneath.

Where on the enchantment
Of romance
For apprehension to step aside,
Place a wish upon a silver coin
Dropped into the gentle ripples,
Make a dream come true.

Beneath a heavenly sky
Embraced in each other's arms
To fill the mind with passion,
Bring together body and soul
For hearts to beat the faster,
While standing on the bridge of
Love's Desire.

Masquerade of Love

You ask me to forgive you
Take another chance,
But from your own lips
I've heard these lies before,
All was never what it seemed,
For you were seeing someone else,
Having learnt by my mistakes,
Without trust there is no love at all.

You've played the game,
Bent the rules, to suit your self,
Become a joker in a pack of cards.
So turn about, walk the other way,
Find another fool to get taken in
While I step aside,
Without trust there is no love at all.

In the masquerade of love
One day someone will come along
To sweep you off your feet,
For you to take off your mask,
Find no one there,
Having learnt too late, without trust
There is no love at all,
For they will have been wearing
A mask themselves.

Heart of Stone

I gave you my love
But you never gave it in return:
I tried so hard to win you over,
Make you understand
How love was meant to be,
But your mind was beyond
The reach of touch,
For your heart was made of stone.

While I was building castles in the air
You were on a distant cloud,
To leave me in the dark
Searching for that spark
To set a flame alight,
But romance had no place.

I tried to find a way,
A key to unlock your heart,
But it was never there to find.
To stand alone
With pity, pouring down the rain.

When I kissed you
The magic wasn't there,
All it did was to leave me in despair
Thinking I was the guilty one,
Instead all the while
The answer lay with you.

With my arms around you
Looking at a starry sky
You froze on ice
In a world of your own:
For how can one melt
A heart made of stone?

Red Roses

Before you send red roses
Make me understand
That your love is sincere,
For I've been hurt
Having been taken in before.

Fill my mind with the truth
Upon words of love:
To cancel out those said
On lips that lied.

Make me trust again
Believe in what you say is true:
On a kiss with emotion
That comes from the heart.

Before you send red roses
Make me feel how much you care
That I'm special in your life,
With no one else you'd rather be.

For should this foolish heart
Throw caution to the wind,
Take another chance,
Only for fate
Stare me in the face again.

Before you send red roses
Make me understand
That your love is sincere,
For I've been hurt,
Having been taken in before.

Foot Note:

With tears of joy in my eyes,
Thank you for the lovely red roses.

Under a Cloud to Hide the Moon

If only I could have read your mind
From the start,
Before you left me cold
With a shiver on the heart,
Under a cloud to hide the moon.

Why did you deceive me
By thinking we had it all?
But it was only make-believe,
Deceit beneath a pretty face:
Leave me in a one-sided love affair
That never stood a chance.

On a wake-up call that came too late
To count the days, you wasted of my life
In believing every word you said was true:
Why couldn't you have been straight
Before I fell in love with you?
Leave me in a one-sided love affair
That never stood a chance.

I'm taking a one-way ticket
To where I can't be found,
Say goodbye to what might been,
Kick-start my life again, somewhere new,
Leave a tear on the past
With this thought of you:

If only I could have read your mind
From the start,
Before you left me cold
With a shiver on the heart,
Under a cloud, to hide the moon.

Writing's on the Wall

I know by your touch
My senses tell me so,
But you haven't got the nerve
To give it to me straight,
End this pretence
That you don't love any more.
Turn around, to not look back,
See the writing's on the wall.

On meaningless words
That my heart believed in,
Upon the stain of tears
Drenched in sorrow
To turn the other cheek
Not having seen before
The writing was on the wall.

Forgive Me

Forgive me if I say I love you
But you don't feel the same,
Just walk away, leave me behind
Before the hurt begins
To rest a troubled mind,
Hello becomes goodbye:
Your face just a memory in time.

In fondness not in hate,
Greet you in the street on a smile,
Of having known you once.
Not to pass you by, though
I never knew your name.

Forgive me if say I love you.
Tell me you feel the same,
Don't walk away, leave me behind,
Having found the key to romance:
To fill our minds with joy,
Hearts with ecstasy.

One Day at a Time

On the shadows of yesterday.
Sleeps the night on hope:
Wake up on the light of tomorrow,
Take one day at a time.

Troubles will always find you
No matter, ever which way you turn:
For there's always someone out there
Ready to pull your world apart.

You think you've got it altogether
When just around the corner,
Some chap is selling broken dreams:
Forewarn you that life is never simply
Black and white, but the grey between.

Life's walking down a one-way street
With no other path to take:
No turning back, to rectify mistakes,
At journey's end to be revealed,
The greatest secret ever kept:
Is there life after death?

On the shadows of yesterday,
Sleeps the night on hope:
Wake up on the light of tomorrow,
Take one day at a time.

Words of a Down and Out

Looking at me now, mate,
You wouldn't think that once
I was an up and coming artist,
But that was long ago.
Now I paint graffiti
On blank walls
Where ever I can find one,
Then piss up against them
To relieve self-pity.

In depths of degradation
I drink far too much
To become paranoid,
Try to drown my sorrows
In my own vomit,
Then on pegs of remorse
Hang myself out to dry.

I had the gift of words once
Now gathering dust
In the corner of my mind,
For then swiftly flowed the pen.
Could have won a Nobel Prize,
Become a Poet Laureate,
Get buried, in Westminster Abbey.
But fame was never meant to be.

My arms are like pin cushions
I got hooked on effin' drugs,
Sorry to waste your time, mate.
See you down the cemetery.

Walking the Pavement

You walk the pavement on a stroll
In the early hours
After midnight,
Of town all boarded up
Forlorn in the gloom of
A few remaining street lights,
Sentries on guard
Just in case you get the inclination,
Want to steal a falling star.

You come across a down and out
In a shop door way sleeping rough,
With a dog on a rope, by his side
Along with a worn out blanket
To keep him warm,
Who shouts out aloud!
Waking up the nesting birds around:
'Have you got a light mate?'
To give him a box of matches,
Along with a couple of fags.

With a nod of the head, walk on by.
On a distance between
To stop in your tracks,
Upon a cry of an ambulance
In the direction from whence you came,
Quickly retrace your steps
See the down and out on stretcher
Being taken away in an ambulance
Say to yourself, 'Poor sod, he'll be D.O.A.'

Taken aback
You grip a hand into a fist
Give yourself a talking-to,
In thinking how lucky you are
Not to be in dire straits,
Having a home to go back to,
Holding a rope,
With a dog trailing on behind.

Someone Like You

You are like a vintage wine
That goes straight to the head:
A song that lingers on the mind,
Repeating the words
Long after they've been said.

To be bewitched under a spell
Of old black magic:
With the more I see you
Stronger love becomes,
For my mind to be filled with delight
On the moment you appear in sight.

Send a shock wave straight
To the heart,
Leave me mystified in thinking
Like quicksilver through my fingers,
You'll just disappear.

Strange to say, I've never felt
This way before,
Love that was misty is now so clear:
Though until now I've been waiting
For the curtains to be drawn back
Upon the stage of love.

Fascination

On the fascination of your smile
Spellbound, time stood still,
To bend the light through the prism
Of love,
Where no words need to be said
For feelings say it all.

With an outgoing tide,
See your face reflected
In a placid pool left behind.
For seahorses to ride the waves,
Upon the fascination of your smile.

In the fall of an April shower
With laughter in your eyes
See you dance beneath,
For the clouds to go drifting by
The sun to open up the sky,
Upon the fascination of your smile.

For the chalice of love
To overflow with joy,
Jealousy to step aside
While pity dries its tears of sorrow
Upon the fascination of your smile.

Long Before I Saw You

Long before I saw you
Long before I met you
To know with fate to guide me,
I would find the one and only you.

Then on a chance encounter
You came to pass my way,
Gave me the eye
While I looked you up and down:
To know at moment's glance
My search was over,
I had found the one and only you.

You were so enchanting
With a look that entranced the mind:
So easy to get to know,
For the closeness to be already there
Though we had never been apart,
For come what may
To share all our tomorrows
With the love we found that day.

Long before I saw you
Long before I met you
To know with fate to guide me,
I would find the one and only you.

My Heart Didn't Need to Tell Me

My heart didn't need to tell me
What I already knew,
For I was never more sure in life
Than when I fell in love with you.

For what I wouldn't give,
To relive those magic moments
In the splendour of those days
I spent with you.

From that moment we first met
We were drawn together
By that sensation that came within,
To know that once in time
Would never, come again.

Those vintage years of sparkling wine
Embracing the thrill of romance,
Stay forever young at heart
With happiness upon the face.

For what I wouldn't give
To relive those magic moments,
In the splendour of those days
I spent with you.

My heart didn't need to tell me
What I already knew,
For I was never more sure in life
Than when I fell in love with you.

Come with Me, My Love

Come with me, my love,
To know when we're together,
The feeling of belonging
That comes within.

On a clear day
Take me by the hand,
Climb a mountain high:
From its summit in the sky,
See paradise lost
Waiting to be found.

When day is done, lie with me
Through the shades of night:
To find you still in my arms
When dawn begins to break.

Come with me, my love.
In our place in time, walk together
Until life's journey's end:
There to find the path of eternal love.

Miss Tinkle Toes

Mia, Mia, little Mia,
Wants to be a dancer
Just like her nana was,
On her toes, she twirls around,
Pirouettes in time with a ballerina
On a wound-up music box,
Going round and round.

With taps on her shoes,
Dances to the rhythm
Of a blind jazz player,
Reading the notes from his mind,
To rattle the black and white keys
Syncopating with his fingers
His given gift in life.

Mia, Mia, little Mia,
I see you growing up
More like your nana, day by day,
So dance, Miss Tinkle Toes,
And never stop,
To fulfil your dreams,
Become a dancer
Like your nana did.

The Dread of Cancer

Silently unseen creeps cancer's deadly path,
Leaving in its wake fear to tremble,
While grief cries its mournful tears.

It robbed you of that carefree smile
That once I knew so well upon your face,
Deprived you of the pride taken,
In your lovely flowing hair,
That was so soft, unto the touch.
To make you, in your utmost despair,
Reverse the mirror of reflection.

For cancer, with its stranglehold on life,
To stay illusive, unrelenting:
In trepidation, stand helplessly aside,
Watch happiness lose all meaning:
Hide its smile behind gathering clouds of dread.
While in the path of sadness, blight the meadow of
All future dreams, to lay the dust.

With hope, trembling on a prayer, of make-believe,
Felt the bitter taste of death, upon my tongue.
In my unstable state, for day to eclipse with night,
When on a shudder, for mercy, to cry out loud within:
'Let it be, let it be, let go, that she might sleep in peace,
Where angels rest their wings and cancer can reach her
No more.'

So it was, in my arms, on the sigh of that last kiss:
To close her eyes, with the serenity of peace upon her face.
For sadness to dwell within the mind:
Turn the hourglass upside down,
Think on cherished memories, untouched by hand, nor time.
Leaving me to say, to all those out there, that share my grief,
Remember this: 'You do not cry alone.'

Living with Cancer

In an off-the-shoulder robe,
Naked she stands in front of
A cheval standing mirror,
Not in the need of being reminded
Of thoughts branded on the mind,
But finding the courage
In coming to terms with.

With her fingertips
To gently touch the scars
Left behind.
Quickly cover them up from sight,
On turning point in time.

Listening to her subconscious mind
Each day, acceptance grows
A little stronger,
On seeing her infant granddaughter,
Seated at the dressing table mirror,
Using make-up in a slapstick manner,
Gives a faint glimmer of a smile
Thinking, *she looks a lot like me*.

With a finger to her lips, to silent the thought,
'I do so hope I'll see her grow up to be
A young lady,
Dear God, I'd settle for that.'
With a flash of light, flick of the finger,
For a moment, she was that little girl herself.

White Feathers

With the breath of life diminishing,
For peace and quiet
Pat, my wife, had been moved
To the single Snow Drop room,
Adjacent to the cancer ward.

For on suppressed tears,
To tightly hold her hand
Not wishing to let go:
While the candle of life
Flickered on the words, in a whisper,
'I love you.'

With pepped-up emotion,
In broad daylight,
I drove through a cloud of white feathers
With some remaining on the windscreen,
To having been no illusion.

Arriving home,
On putting a key in the door
To be confronted by a white dove inside,
On the ledge behind a glass pane
Of the front bay window.

Instantly thinking, it had fallen down the chimney,
To hurriedly let myself in:
Where gentle, though a babe in a peaceful sleep,
Let me hold it, to open up a window
See it soar into the sky, of the heavens above.
On the next morning to wonder if I had been dreaming,
Only to find a white feather on the floor, by the window:
For true love to have no bounds.

Why Does It Have to Be?

Why does it have to be
You were taken away from me?
When in life there was
So much more love to give:
For time to only weep
Sleep the pain of sorrow.

Echo the valleys and hills,
Run the rivers deep with tears
To flood into the sea,
For a love that once we knew.

Why does it have to be?
While memories cling the ivy,
In remembrance of those days
Silence speaks a kiss.
For in love's remorse
The sun to eclipse the moon
In the loneliness of time unlived.

Echo the valleys and hills,
Run the rivers deep with tears
To flood into the sea,
For a love that once we knew.

If Only

If only we could have met
In the long ago:
Before the moss grew
Over the flowers that never bloomed:
Between the now and then
To say I love you
On all those years we never knew.

For life together was too short
To take the wonder of you from sight:
Leave me with the thought
I knew a true love that went so deep.

If only we could have shared
Time together:
That slipped away before
Our eyes saw one another:
All those unlived dreams
Which faded into the mist:
Between the now and then
To say I love you on all those years
We never knew.

For life together was too short
To take the wonder of you from sight:
Leave me with the thought
I knew a true love that went so deep.

Every Now and Then

Every now and then
On the spirit of the wind,
In a whisper of your voice
To send an echo through
The passage of my mind.

On closed eyes
In my imagination
See your face before me,
Reach out my hands to hold you
Only to touch thin air.

Though an angel from above,
You tiptoe through a pale moonlight,
Leave a kiss upon the pillow,
Then vanish back into
The folds of night,
Feel your presence come and go.

Every now and then
I hear your cry, upon that moment,
Of that last kiss, to say goodbye.
Our tears to weep the willow
While in remembrance of your love,
To remain between the pages in
The hours of a prayer.

You Were Love

You were love
In all its splendour,
With the gaiety of a child
Full of laughter on a swing.
That special gift of joy
I found in happiness
In knowing you,
On the fringe of heaven
Fulfilment within a dream.

To kiss you on an April shower,
Felt the glow of tenderness within
Beneath a June day sun,
Glory in all its majestic colours
Of an autumn's fall,
To wrap you in my arms
Against winter's
Bitter winds of snow,
For you were love alone.

In the Ashes of Our Love

In the ashes of our love,
On the shadows of the past,
It's not easy to come to terms
Loneliness dragging its heels,
For life without a purpose
Can be no life at all.

It's not easy on the conscience
To take another chance,
When you've already
Lost the emotions
Say lies on words
Having lost their meanings

With the touch of their lips,
To close the eyes in thinking
I was kissing you.
For every which way I turn
You are always there beside me.

In the nearness of you
Having left my love burning
An eternal flame:
In the ashes of our love,
Upon shadows of the past.

Images of Love

Spring was my darling
When May blossom
Wore its bridal gown,
Peeped the bud to bloom
In shyness of the sun,
Fall softly the rain
On images of love.

Summer was my darling
When clover on the field,
Blushed the cheek
In pink caress,
Buttercups in shyness
Flirted with the daisies,
Fall softly the shadows
On images of love.

Winter was my darling
When holly's berries
Hung the bough,
Church bells rung
Across fields of white,
To hide the green
Of a summer gone.
Fall softly the snow
On images of love.

Reminiscence

When hand in hand, we strolled beneath
A canopy of magnolia blossom in full bloom,
Where upon a gentle breeze, take in its fragrance,
While listening to the bells that rung out
From a distant church
That resounded across a clear blue sky.
To be spellbound by the magic in the air,
Love to show its face in all its splendour.

With you wrapped in my arms, dreamy-eyed,
Watch an evening sun fall into the sea.
For an umber moon take its place, in a celestial sky.
On a changing tide, for the waves to come rolling in
Gently kiss the shore:
Wash away our footprints in the sand,
For secrets told, whispering the shells.

On the last day of a summer's evening,
To waltz the night away, beneath a chandelier of stars,
Fall asleep, locked in each other's arms,
In a dream dance the edge of the moon.
Wake to find within, that peace of mind
On the joy that happiness brings.

Of Autumn's calling, the leaves were falling,
In their glory, lay a carpet of red and gold.
See in your eyes happy laughter
Remembering those days when a child:
For together, holding hands
To chase the falling leaves that danced,
On a gentle breeze, along the ground.

When snow flakes fell all around,
With shutters closed against the windows,
To keep out the wind that howled, like a wolf on the prowl.
While we laid curled up, beside an open fire's glow,
That flickered to dance upon the ceiling:
With you in my arms,
Softly I read love poems aloud.

Painted Pictures on the Mind

I rowed the boat with oars
Rippling the reflection of the sun,
While you trailed your hand
In the waters drifting by,
Watched by a kingfisher
Perched upon a branch
Above the reeds.

Fusion of love and emotion
Painting pictures on the mind
In reflection of past time,
While sitting in a rocking chair
Upon the meadow of bygone dreams.

On that spring time
With joy of laughter upon your face,
Shoes in hand in bare feet
See you tripping amongst the bluebells
Beneath the trees, in the splendour of
Their spring leaves.

When hand in hand
In an evening stroll
To the sound of a church choir,
For the moon to glow in your green eyes
Fill my mind with thoughts of love
Kiss you on thanksgiving of a prayer.

Fusion of love and emotion
Painting pictures on the mind
In reflection of past time,
While sitting in a rocking chair
Upon the meadow of bygone dreams.

Tragedy of War: WWI

Half-empty pubs, mournful streets,
Missing the lads
That cheerfully volunteered,
Went off to war:
In hindsight not knowing then
How many would return,
In one state, or another
On minds torn asunder.

For a country to be in total mourning,
On blinds pulled down and curtains drawn.
Far more in number then those untouched
While women all dressed in black
Tried to come to terms with their loss:
Console themselves in prayer,
Reading pages from the bible.

Girlfriends jilted by death
Left childless
Watch those playing in the streets,
That would grow up
Never knowing their dad.

In the aftermath of war
Endless lines of wooden crosses,
Amongst the bloodstained
Tissue, paper poppies:
In a debt of dedication
For the blood spilt by gallant men.
On the call of the bugle,
Laid down their lives:

To place upon regimental flags
Further battles fought and won.
While the glorious dead
March behind the drummer boy
Killed at Waterloo.

The Conscript

With pals of mine
Stripped to the waist:
To stand in line
On a medical parade,
To drop your pants and cough:
Should nothing fall off
You're A1, mate.

The recruiting sergeant said:
Doesn't matter if
You can't read, nor write,
To fire a rifle, just imagine
You're shooting a target at the fair,
Instead of taking home
A stuffed teddy bear:
A nice shiny medal to wear.

We Were the Young Lads

We were the young lads
Bold with pride, fearless in our prime.
With a stride in our step
Walked down the streets of home.

For then time was on our side
The future was never ours to know,
Only destiny could tell, waiting to unfold.

We were the young lads
With the world at our feet,
Flirted with the girls,
To find out, what love could be about.

For then time was on our side
The future was never ours to know,
Only destiny could tell, waiting to unfold.

We were the young lads
With spirit, rebellious in our ways,
Ready to stand up for our rights,
Make the world a better place.

For then time was on our side
The future was never ours to know,
Only destiny could tell, waiting to unfold.

We were the young lads
With courage in our hearts,
Ready to prove our worth,
Fight for freedom, love and glory.

For then time was on our side
The future was never ours to know,
Only destiny could tell, waiting to unfold.

We were the young lads
That heard the call to arms,
Went off to war, but never came back.
With a stride in our step
Walk down the streets of home, no more.

For now time was no longer on our side.
Destiny had been told,
The path of glory ours to tread
Heaven was ours to know.

One in Khaki, One in Grey

Two soldiers stand in different lands,
One in khaki, one in grey,
Unknown in face, unknown in name,
In prayer they kneel to pray.

Somewhere a field,
Grass still green, not trodden by war,
Scared by shell, nor trench:
Where silence awaited the thunder of hell
To turn it into a battlefield,
Tear apart the peace of a quiet countryside.

Another phase of history set
Valour's glory to enact:
In the halls of immortality
Already veiled the names,
Of those that were to die.

Up to the front-line they came
One in khaki, one in grey
To face each other across no man's land:
Wait their fate, call of duty.

Suddenly firing ceased, all was still:
Deferred their butchery,
Christ had laid his hand upon the soil
For it was Christmas morn.
Came together, one in khaki, one in grey,
Known in face, known in name,
Goodwill towards all men.

Their encounter brief,
Positions taken up once more,
But hope remains, even in a time of war
Love is stronger than hate.
Somewhere a field,
Where the grass is green again
Peace returned, to a quiet countryside.

Pawns of Grief

Turned the soil
Dug the trench:
Unearthed beetle
Devil's advocate
In solemn wait:
To slide the depth of
Slaughter's aftermath.

In played-out sadness
Of souls held to ransom:
See young happy heart
Seal his fate
To tarnish glory,
Dull the jewel of youth:
Across cemeteries' acres
Lay the pawns of grief.

Red Runs the Sky

On fixed bayonets
Forward went reluctant heroes,
Straight into direct line of fire upon
Fritz's glare:
Looking down the sights of
A machine-gun's barrel.

In an effigy of war, possessed scythe
Mowed down the lads
In corn's reflection,
Locust to reap the harvest
Of future seeds for sewing:
A deserted playground,
Where no children play
Or laugh at Punch and Judy
At the sands.

Pressed blistered heel in soil to flake
This domicile not of their choosing,
Too late shepherd's warning
Penned and slaughtered the flock,
Red runs the sky with blood.

Rain Marks Time

Waiting on the signal of command
In the trenches
Lined the soldiers with their rifles:
To bite the lip to hold back fear
On the shrill note of whistle's blast
For over the top went the lads.

Stretched forth
An unconsummated graveyard
Whose open jaws, cried out for more:
In sympathy with lives to be taken
For the sun to hide behind the clouds,
While the rain came down, in drips of pit-a-pat.

Kill, kill, and kill again
If you survive my lad, you'll be a bloody hero:
But will your mind the horror to forget?
In a generation yet to come:
Legless beggar, with ribbons vanished,
Blame left behind, those that cared, buried
For only the rain marks time, with sleeping souls.

Demons in Grey

Through eerie smog
In hideous masks,
Reincarnated, devils in disguise
Forward came the Boche,
Assassins, ghosts in grey.

Ill-equipped to be robbed of sight
With pals of mine:
Cough and choke on gas
To retreat,
Flounder in our tracks
In a disorderly disarray.

On eyes wrapped up, in single files,
Hands on the shoulders of
The one in front,
To be led away:
For 'Blind Man's Bluff' is no game.

Ceasefire

Speechless guns, hushed by a truce,
To collect the dead
That had been left behind:
A time to pinch oneself
Make sure that you're still alive,
Puff on a woodbine, scribble a letter home.

Stretcher-bearers forward
To walk and stumble amongst
The countless, littered bodies:
Tread on limbs torn apart
Trodden into the mud, in time
To be turned over by the plough,
For on tomorrow, guns to roar again.

Unknown Perils

Tragedy echoes the labyrinth
Of unknown perils,
Bat to rest the shoulder
On night's quivering breath,
Creep shadows in undulating patterns,
On a weary soldier's sight.

Taunt the mind on hell's awakening,
Triggers tension's trembling hand,
All life chilled on edge of death,
Valiant to be the brave,
Else coward lay the trench.

Silent Harp

When first we marched up to the front
On swinging arms, feet in step,
Singing musical hall songs of the day
Unaware of what lay ahead?
Naive, ignorant in the experience of war:
Innocence irretrievable,
Gone with the first taking of life.

While blood and sweat fill the eyes,
For compassion, to tremble on the mind:
No signposts pointing back to home,
Reprieve for a dissolution soldier:
So against all odds, on fear to wipe my brow
Stand fast with fellow compatriots,
To die tomorrow if spared today:
In trepidation, hear the sound of the silent harp.

Prince of Youth

Wrapped up in barbed wire's thorns
See the prince of youth:
Though a sculpture's effigy
Tragedy of war.

Lifeless limbs, their last mile ran,
Coils metal's wreath,
On death's stark bush
Blood cold, on point of nail.

Silenced the bee on nettle's sting,
Poppy to claim the wild rose
On bramble's thorn,
In the dying of his day
England's prince of youth.

Virgin Snowdrop

Torn asunder, young was the soldier
Virgin snowdrop, trampled on glory's path,
Trespassed on death before its calling
Sings a lullaby, where no armies march.

Spirit of a tiger, crawled the devil's mask,
Smothered child in blanket of gas
To find safety, in eternal sleep
In nursery's garden, sweet lays the peace.

Son of Love

Son of love
War the face to change,
Distort the mind
Cancel out the peace,
In wait you sit the trench
For all that gentle thought
To stare the mud.

Faint sound upon the ear
Of summer's thrush,
Whistles death's cry
In bullets' mould shape,
Eternal sleep to come
Before the nightingale
Is heard.

No more the torments of hell
For you my lad,
But what inscription
Shall we give thee
Upon the plaque
In the church of the choir
Where you sung?

Simply here dwells the spirit of
'The son of love'.

Forever Young

Upon his rifle rests his helmet
Beneath he lays forever young:
In the spring of his years
Green of youth days,
On hope triumphant:
Sleeps his head the pillow of sorrow.

Mind clear in crystal stream,
Voice gentle in choir sounding:
Mellowing of outrage not for him.
Schoolboy dreams never faded,
Free in spirit, gay in laughter,
Too old to be a child, too young to be wise.

Sweet smile of innocence,
Carefree eyes of joy,
Age not his concern:
Heart full of love, for lovers he never knew,
Truth still upon the lips,
Lies of falsehood undisturbed:
Cold contempt of misspent hours
Not his worry.

Unlived memories,
To die in the ashes of his life.
Seasons to seasons
Flowers to flowers
Leaves to leaves
Never to grow old.

Love Instead of Hate

Cradles the soil, of an unknown soldier,
Smile that captured boyhood revelry
Laid to waste on dead tomorrows.

Maggot to crawl the eye of rotting flesh,
Whose sight once saw
May buds blooming:
Still within the chrysalis
The wings summer's calling.

Bowed shame in sins confessed,
Pence of the guilty, yet to be resolved:
To count the seasons of the years
In wait to cancel out all wars,
Speak of love, instead of hate.

Path of Eagles

Fear grows with dwindling ranks
Cheats the devil life,
But not the soul:
Worn-out boots to march
In step to glory.

Finger of faith pointing to heaven:
Golden Fleece entwined the gorse
Tolls softly the bell,
While murmurs the heart.

For tranquilly to lay the threshold
Of the gates to heaven:
Sunday morn comes home
To weekday's child,
Dove to the fly the path of eagles.

Where No Birds Sing

No birds sing across death's stretch of
Fallen comrades,
Autumn's fall, leaves from mighty oak,
Where stemmed Motherland's
Future generation
To rest her sons on foreign soil,
In their demise, weep a generation
Never to be born.

Age upon the face before its time.
Murmurs voices of their injustice
Of the days they never knew,
The air they never breathed:
Nor to lie beneath the skies of home,
For only crucified scarecrows
Guard the fields, where no birds sing.

Fields of Sorrow/Fields of Glory

Poets lay dead
Before words could be written,
Artists' blood split
On a blank canvas, to congeal.
Composer an unfinished symphony
Last movement,
A eulogy set to music
Played on a mouth organ.

Craftsmen's tools
Exchanged for weapons of war,
Blacksmith's forge
The sunset of evening.
Forester gone to attend trees
In the valley beyond.

Lawyer closing his case
On an open verdict of death,
Chaplin defending
His faith to the end.
Steeplejack
Climbed glory's descent
Placed the flag of freedom
On the pinnacle,
Of the kingdom of heaven.

All walks of life
Came in their thousands,
Laid down their lives
For king and country,
To rest the battlefields
Of unrelated turf.

Requiem

In communion's chalice
Drips the blood
Of human sacrifice,
For on a hymn
Earth finds heaven,
The moon in waiting
To sleep the dead.

No fertile womb
To conceive
No child to bear
His name,
When poppies bloom again
In requiem sing his praise.

Village Memorial

Where stands the war memorial
Now just names stare the green:
That once saw the light,
Bowled the ball, cracked the bat.

Run out lives
Before their inning's complete
To never see the final score of victory:
But won the day upon
The crease of freedom
Of England's playing fields.

The Barley Field

On the shadows of darkness, pulled back the curtains
Of night:
For the sun, to break through the clouds,
Kiss the barley field below, that sways to and fro,
Though waves upon a placid sea.

Where stands, nearby, a mighty oak, reaching for the sky
While clings the ivy to its bark, clutching onto secrets,
That time has left behind:
To impart in whispers, on the silence of the air:
Down the rows, to where the barley grows.

When in, bygone days, the land was ploughed:
By horse and man, reins in hand.
Where happy, laughing children played, holding hands,
Across the barley:
Run up and down the rows, while it grew, to ripen in the sun.

Where from the village pavilion, now in disrepair,
Echo in the shadows, memories of
Those glories, hot summer days, when on the village green
To cheers of overwhelming joy, young Henry Brown
Hit the ball for six, time after time.

On hearts, carved into the bark of oak, to name but one:
Jenny Lyn, who got married in the village church,
To John O'Neal, before going off to war:
Little knowing then, he'd be dead, before their baby cried,
Dread of the telegraph boy, to come knocking at the door.

Cries an owl to summons, an evening sky:
For on the twilight, bring to an end, another day.
Sleep the past of yesterday, on the dawning of tomorrow.
When further secrets to impart, until the time to harvest,
Down the rows, to where the barley grows

Remembrance Day

Breaks the wake of dawn, heralding morning's light,
For the frozen tears of dew, to cry a bloodshot sky,
While hushed the wind that tossed the poppies:
In dedication of this day, given to honour the fallen,
Of the two great wars:
That laid down their lives for: 'King and Country'.

On past moments, for those that never came back.
To rest beneath the skies of home:
With all hope gone, grieve to cry in pain, forever more.
In solitude the betrothed, veiled in black, instead of white:
Mourned seeds unsown, weep a generation never born,
To follow on, the family name.

Where hanged a wreath upon the door, with curtains drawn:
For a fair maiden in distress, to kneel beside, place flowers on
An unmarked grave.
In the course of time with age, to put a face, weep a name,
Etched upon a war memorial stone:
For pity, to encroach, on how life could have been.

In present moments of this day, for the shrill notes of a bugle,
To tremble across an open sky:
Send a shiver down the spine, weld a tear on bowed heads,
Deep in thought, on reflections, of how it must have been:
When duty called, on the edge of fear, to sacrifice,
God's precious gift of life,

On every 'Remembrance Sunday' to unite a proud nation,
In the two-minute silence, devoted to prayer:
While from heaven, souls of the brave look down,
Lest we forget the price of freedom, in the air we breathe.

THE LOST LETTERS
(SET TO POETRY)

When First We Met

With open arms, I'd run to meet you,
On the laughter in your eyes
To swing me round:
With the sound of the cuckoo
Chase me through woods
Find my hiding place.

At harvest time, to gather up the straw,
Make mischief in the hay stacks:
To leave behind stubble fields
In waiting of next spring,
For the March hares to cavort again.

Where beneath the trees
We sheltered from the rain,
Watched through the glistening leaves
The sun to break through in dappled light:
With only love to crowd the mind
For you to kiss me,
Prickle the skin, in love sublime:
Leave no doubt within the mind
I had fallen madly in love with you.

When the Days Were Ours

In gaslight's umber glow, lace-wing flies
Recalling melodies
That danced the carousel,
Twisted brass, polished to gleam,
Fashioned wood, white horses to ride:
With not a care,
For gay was the laughter, upon my lips
When the days were ours, moments shared,
Now lonely I am without thee.

At Summer Leighton, fantailed the doves,
With the twirl upon a parasol,
Straw hat that chequered the light
Upon my face.
With a carefree smile, hand in hand
For only joy to tempt a tear,
While we strolled its stately grounds.
When the days were ours, moments shared,
Now to weep in fear without thee.

Whisperings

On a gentle breeze
Of a summer's evening:
Sounds an orchestra
Rustling of leaves:
Whispering secrets told
In the dying embers
Of the day.

Sings a nightingale
On a church flint wall:
While spoken words of love
For the heart to tremble
Upon the touch of the lips
Surrender of a kiss.

Skims white owl
Across the lonely fields,
To greet the night once more
With its haunting call:
Return to lover's sanctuary.

Together We Will Be

Though the months have gone,
Last year's leaves still remain
Huddling the ground
Where our footsteps trod:
A remainder of unforgettable days
That was the summer of our lives.

Now I walk the woods alone,
Talking to myself, though you were
By my side,
Holding onto fragile memories
That crinkle fragile edge
Of crumbling leaf.

Dear Jonathan,
Your presence sadly missed,
With the exchange
Of flannel and tweed
For khaki green:
Sunburnt face lost its colour
Since you went away.

I've lit so many candles
Said so many prayers,
My mind is numb:
The heart drained
To cry more tears,
For overflows the cup of love.

Yesterdays

I miss you so
Now brambles cover
Footpath made through bluebell wood
Primroses have shown their face again,
So I will lend my thoughts
To a year gone by,
When the yesterdays
Were full of hope and meaning.

Cornflowers perfume the air again
When hand in hand
I knew the closeness of your touch,
So I will lend my thoughts
To a year gone by,
When the yesterdays
Were full of hope and meaning.

I will be sad to hear September's song,
See the birds migrating,
For the shades of evening to quickly fall,
So I will lend my thoughts
To a year gone by,
When the yesterdays
Were full of hope and meaning.

Buttercup Meadow

Fair summer gone
Eyes that shone with laughter
When all life burst into a celandine
Dear touch
That made this heart tremble
Cannot one forget-me-not
Remember in the echo of those days?

I close my eyes, see you before me
When with a chuckle
Called me freckle face
Shouted out loud you loved me
To shake the buttercups,
Fill my heart with aspiration
But on a shiver you are gone
For on the meadow
The sun is cold this day.

Winter Lace

Remember the days
With joy in our hearts
Played merry the tune
Romance was in the making,
Love's waiting game
Floated the swan,
For how long will it be
Before you hold me, kiss me again?

Feel the beating of your heart
In unison with mine,
For with your arms around
Feel safe again,
Tears of sadness no more to cry
But with time passing by,
Feel wearing black winter lace
Will be my valentine.

Sweet Marjorie

When crying comes
Lips no more to speak the kiss,
Faded my presence
Thoughts with you remain:
Remember, sweet Marjorie,
Did not we live,
Those moments well we shared?

On death's collapsed carousel
Colour turns to pale:
Life stops breathing, drawing to its close,
Extinguished by an enemy
I never knew,
To harbour the bitter taste of hate.

Why must it be I die alone
To rest an unknown cross,
When someone knew me well
Upon my days?
Yet in the sadness of it all
We found love's meaning:
Remember, sweet Marjorie,
Did not we live,
Those moments well we shared?

Until We Meet Again

Dear Marjorie, wait not for my return,
For swiftly cast the shadows
Upon the light, to dim my eyes,
On time remaining
My thoughts rest with you.

Those tender moments shared,
Hearts to tremble
On the lingering of a kiss,
To know that once in time
Was ours to share
That no one else can take away.

Dear Marjorie, upon your lips
My kiss remains
Until we meet again, in the bounds
Of a world beyond
For my memory to stay save
Within your heart, for ever more.

Killed in Action

Worst fears confirmed.
In the solitude of grief
From my window
I see one magpie instead of two:
To close my eyes
Touch your lips with icy fingers,
On tears, cry out your name.

If only you had been reported missing
Hope would still remain,
But killed in action is unrepentant
To close the book of life:
Leave only memories to remain.

So my love, my dearest love,
I need a purpose, for I am lost in sorrow:
Having decided to devote life
In becoming a suffragette.
For on this November morn
With my coat collar turned up
Your presence beside me
Walk together down our lane to Freshenfield.

Will You Remember Me

Who speaks the silence of the dead
Murmuring of the poppies on the wind?
Years denied the joys of living,
Yours was the dying, but mine are the prayers.

In thought, with you I sleep the night,
Touching the dawn of tomorrow:
With your presence denied
Not sharing the light of day.

Remorseful in mind, for my thoughts
To lay by your side,
In time to be reunited in the eyes of God,
When I will remember you the way you were,
Will you remember me, the way I shall be?
Yours was the dying, but mine are the prayers.

In Remembrance

I am the wingless butterfly,
An empty shell void of life,
A tree without its leaves
Looking to the sky,
Searching for answers
That will never be forthcoming,
Why I should lose you in this way?

Should in another life
I find you once again,
My selfish heart would weep,
These arms enfold you tightly
To never let you go,
For war to deny us of our love.

Skeleton of Despair

A voice in a whisper comes stealing
Through the edge of night,
To call upon your ears
The listening of words.
Mine was the divine time
That knew your beauty
On the crest of youth,
To gaze upon your smile
With the summer on your face,
Now lays the thoughts
My soul to cry,
In death's valley of the fallen.

With a kiss, concealed from sight
To touch your lips with tender love,
Upon a wish, if only I could share
That comfort of your bed.
Oh joy, where is your laughter now
To cry my soul upon
Those carefree pleasures gone?
Life, wake me not again,
For your reality is too cold in its dying,
To leave behind a skeleton of despair.

Primrose Wood

On stolen hours, seasons denied,
My soul lies dreaming in primrose woods
Beneath a mellow sky:
Watch nature through the seasons
Change its fashion,
While softly treads the deer.

No more for me the burst of shell,
Shrapnel's cry of pain:
On stolen hours, seasons denied,
In the comforting arms of home
My thoughts lay steadfast, undisturbed
Watch the seasons denied
Come and go.

Under the snow of feathery down
I see the green of summers gone,
To think on thoughts of time
That were never ours to know:
For my soul to rest the peace of
Primrose Wood.

About the Author

The author, on finishing college, followed in his chosen career to become a design draughtsman in the field of engineering. Having worked for some major companies, he became a chief draughtsman. Unfortunately, after a bad accident he had to take early retirement.

Having a love for poetry, he started writing it himself, to touch the mind and heart.